Larry on the Loose!

And other Animal Escapades

From the Files of a Humane Educator

Dear Darlene, Jon, Marieko &
Erica &
Almendra,

By Jan Berlin with Lynda Gerenser

Because

Illustrations by Lynda Gerenser

Nice

Cover photographs by Irene Shafer

AND ALL
OF YOU
Matter!!

Edited by Beth Quinn

Love,
Jan

i

Email: janimals@warwick.net

ISBN: 978-1523771783

Preface

"When you grow up and move out of the house, you can have as many animals as you want."

This was my mother's response every time I pleaded with her to let me have a pet – any pet – even a ladybug.

In spite of the house rule against having pets, my mom, Norma Berlin, was the nicest, most compassionate, generous, favorite mom in the neighborhood. She taught me that **nice matters** and instilled in me the values of **respect, kindness, tolerance, compassion and responsibility.** And by not allowing me to have a pet, she probably established within me a foundation for my great desire to have a career working with animals as a humane educator.

As director of Everything Animals Resource & Activity Center, Inc., I now have as many animals as I want (if not more, at times). Most of the animals that have become my ambassadors are rescued critters – animals no longer valued as pets and in need of a new career. When people offer to "donate" an animal to the organization, I first ask if they feel the animal would do well in an educational setting. If the answer is yes then that spider, lizard, opossum or whatever it may be takes on the role of a new ambassador.

I specialize in what many consider unhuggable or unlovable animals. These are animals who might be unattractive, have missing parts, exhibit behavior that's misunderstood and so on. Yet these animals are pure magic for producing an immediate change in attitude. After meeting and learning about these "creepy" ambassadors, audience revulsion is nearly always replaced with compassion – the essence of humane education.

My energies have been so focused on this work that, during a period when I lived in Alaska, I actually commuted from Anchorage to Port Jervis, New York, each month to continue humane education classes in every elementary classroom in that school district. I went to the schools during the week and held a fund raising event for the Humane Society of Port Jervis/Deerpark on Saturdays while in town. I flew back and forth with Pim, a Pomeranian dog, my first official animal ambassador.

In my travels, I have found myself caught in unpredictable situations that proved inconvenient and embarrassing. If you have never had two baby opossums poop in your purse, well … you just haven't lived. A sense of humor helped me get through the many awkward situations that I write about in this book, and I hope you enjoy reading about them as well.

Through the years, I have learned that there can be no ego involved when working with animals. People of all ages come to see what animals are in the various carriers I bring to programs. I offer information and amusement; however, there is no doubt who the stars really are.

- Jan Berlin, February 2016

Contents

This book is dedicated to all who believe that nice really DOES matter.

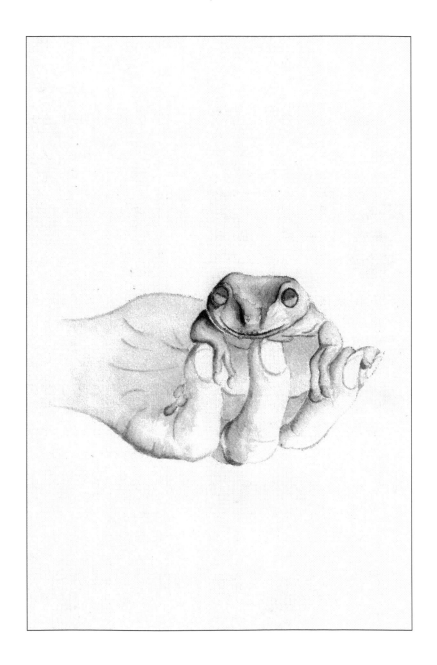

Larry on the Loose

While driving home from a school program in the Detroit area, I opened the pillowcase that was the traveling bag for Larry.

Larry was a sheltopusik, a species of lizard born without limbs. Commonly called legless lizards, they are often mistaken for snakes, and they have the same ability as snakes to creep people out.

Because Larry had been confined for most of the day, I wanted to give him the chance to move around freely in the car. I had a small car and I figured, "How far could he possibly go?"

Well, I found out the answer to *that* question when I got home. Larry was nowhere to be found. I searched every nook and cranny of the car, but ... no Larry. I couldn't imagine how he might have escaped from the car, but I called the Honda dealership to see if there were any holes in the car's design that might serve as an escape hatch for a legless lizard.

They said nope, no escape hatches. I continued my search. I checked under the seats again and again. I looked in the glove compartment. I searched up under the dashboard. No Larry.

I didn't give up hope. The weather was warm, so I left the car windows open a crack for Larry. I put food and water on the floor in hope that he'd be comfortable and well fed until he made a reappearance.

Meanwhile, I had education programs to present and in Larry's absence, I bought a glass lizard as a substitute for the kids to look at. This did not make my boss at Living Science Foundation, where I worked at the time, very happy. In fact, I was strongly lectured about the wisdom – or lack thereof – of allowing animals to roam free in my car. (Actually, to this very day, I have not found anyone who is a fan of my free-roaming policy, so it's altogether possible that my boss was right.)

After two weeks, I gave up hope. I began to expect my car to begin smelling of an animal carcass. But the car's odor remained the same, and I figured – with some degree of hope – that maybe Larry had found a way out of my car after all. I gave up hope of ever seeing him again although I continued to leave food and water in the car.

Around that same time, I needed work done on my car's fan belt, so I made an appointment with a local service station. When I dropped the car off, I didn't bother to mention that an animal might be decaying inside my car or under its hood. I removed the food and water and left the car in the parking lot.

Around mid-day I received a call from the garage. My caller informed that no mechanic would work on my car because there was a snake sitting on the driver's seat.

Apparently, the mechanic had pulled the car halfway into the bay and then got out to do something. When he

Around mid-day I received a call from the service
station. My caller informed that no mechanic would
work on my car because there was a

snake

sitting on the driver's seat.

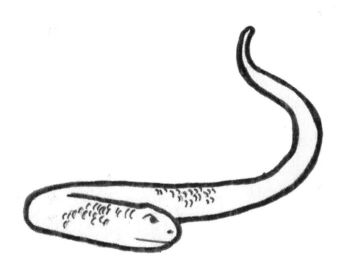

returned to the car THERE WAS LARRY, sitting comfortably on the warm seat!

I was overjoyed and shouted into the phone that it was a legless lizard, not a snake, and that it was totally harmless! The service manager was not impressed with my knowledge of reptiles and repeated that no one would be working on my car until the "snake" was removed. He also said I needed to get there quickly as the car was halfway into the bay and he needed it to be moved.

I got a ride to the garage. When I arrived, to my great relief, there was Larry, relaxing on the dashboard!

I picked him up, offered the mechanics a chance to pet him (they all declined); and gently placed him back into his traveling pouch.

The car was pulled all the way into the garage, the fan belt was fixed and I was able to keep my job.

NOTE: Legless lizards were substituted for snakes in the movie *Raiders of the Lost Ark*.

A Lion in the Office

Those of us who have worked at shelters with open door policies never quite know what will come through that door.

As manager of one of three Michigan Humane Society shelters in 1983, it was my responsibility to care for Nigel, a six-month-old African lion cub who had been taken from a family of three (including a two-year-old child) living in an apartment in Detroit.

Because there was no cage space large enough and far enough away from the public to accommodate a fifty-pound lion cub, Nigel was to live in my office until an appropriate sanctuary could be found.

At first I was excited. I mean, how many people have the opportunity to get close to a lion cub? Nigel was gorgeous and full of personality – he acted like a six-month-old kitten. A fifty-*pound* kitten.

The thing is, anyone who has lived with kittens knows they're maniacs at that age. And Nigel was no different. He jumped up onto furniture as he played. He ran amok. And he chewed on everything that looked tasty or chewy.

When he chewed through the telephone cord of a very new, high-tech (for the 1980s) phone, I couldn't just go out and buy a new one. That's not how it worked in the '80s when phone companies, not stores, provided their customers with phones. When I called the phone service, I explained that I was at the Michigan Humane Society.

"The problem is," I told the company's repair service, "a lion in my office had just chewed through the cord."

"Ha, ha," the person on the phone must have thought. "What jokers those people at the Humane Society are!"

That would explain the shocked look on the repairman's face when he came to install my new phone cord. His face blanched when he opened my office door and saw Nigel sitting there. In fact, he seemed quite shocked.

Well, hadn't I *told* them?!

He stood in the doorway staring at Nigel for a few seconds, then abruptly turned and shut the door. Then he reopened the door and tossed the new phone cord toward me. "You're going to have to do this yourself," he said as he quickly exited the building.

It wasn't all that difficult, actually.

The next time I needed someone to come into my office, I decided to put Nigel in the bathroom for everyone's peace of mind. Unfortunately, the bathroom must have been a pretty boring place for a lion cub to hang out, and Nigel needed some entertainment. Naturally, the best way for a bored lion to pass the time is to gnaw on something tasty or chewy.

When I went to the bathroom to get him, there was Nigel sitting on the floor contentedly chewing on the dislodged toilet seat.

I put a "Standing Room Only" sign on the bathroom door until the seat could be replaced.

Nigel spent the remainder of his time in Michigan at the home of the shelter's executive director. After a huge fund raiser to pay for his airfare, he eventually departed Michigan for Primarily Primates, an animal sanctuary in Texas.

When I went to bathroom to get him, there was Nigel sitting on the floor contentedly chewing on the dislodged toilet seat.

Wacky Bird

When I worked with the Living Science Foundation in Novi, Michigan, one of my favorite animals to bring into the classroom was a Sulfur Crested Cockatoo.

Many years later, when I heard about one that was being displaced due to a divorce, I agreed to adopt Wacky Bird. His name warned of his behavior – a warning I did not heed.

Wacky spent a great deal of time talking to himself. He clearly knew his name, and I often heard him saying, "Wacky Bir-ir-dee," followed by "Wacka-wacka-wacka bir-ir-dee." He'd finished off his pronouncement with, "Wacky, Wacky, Wacky Wacky Birrrrdee."

Then he'd start all over again.

At first it was quite amusing. However, it eventually drove my husband Rich (the world's best sport) and me ... well ... it drove us quite wacky. And those who called on the phone could hear the bird more clearly than they could hear me.

Wacky's sleeping cage was in a room on the first floor of the house. Since most of our time was spent on the second floor, Wacky had a large perch upstairs with us, and he was allowed the run of the upstairs rooms.

He enjoyed sitting on the back of one of the kitchen chairs, which was situated next to a file cabinet. Not a good location. The first time Rich bent over to go into the cabinet, Wacky reached over and bit him on his tush.

Rich was not amused.

Wacky's chair was moved farther from the cabinet. Not a big help. It's amazing how far a cockatoo can stretch his body, neck and head if he wants to bite something! After Rich's second bite, I took Wacky down to his sleeping cage for a time-out. As I carried him downstairs, I said, "Going down, Wacky Bird, going down."

Apparently, the time-out didn't faze him because we went through the same routine again the next day. By the third day, Wacky didn't bother waiting for Rich to bend over. As soon as he saw Rich, he flew down from his chair and started chasing him around the house, pecking at his heels until Rich escaped behind a slammed door.

Clearly, things were not going well with this particular adoption. I continued to bring Wacky upstairs when Rich was not at home so I could give the bird attention during the day, but he remained in his cage downstairs when Rich and his tender tush were home.

One day during this period, I went into the bathroom while Wacky was in the living room. Rich's elderly father, who lived on the first floor of the house, called up to me from the bottom of the stairs.

Dad's hearing was failing, and he couldn't hear me when I yelled down for him to wait a minute because I was in the bathroom. Wacky Bird, apparently sensing the problem, decided to get involved. Thus, our exchange went a bit … wacky.

To speak kindly does not hurt the tongue.

- Proverb

Dad: "Jan!"
Me: "Just a minute, I'm in the bathroom!"
Wacky Bird: "What?"
Dad: "What?"
Wacky: "What?"
Me: "I'm in the bathroom!"
Wacky: "What?"
Dad: "What?"
Me: "I'm in the bathroom!"
Dad and Wacky: "What?"

Eventually, Rich's dad and Wacky quit trying. I guess they were both pretty much talked and squawked out.

Meanwhile, Rich wanted to mend fences with Wacky, and he chose a weekend to bond with the bird when I went to Detroit for a family event. It did not work out as planned.

Rich made an effort. Wacky did not. When the kindly Rich tried to feed Wacky, he was thanked with a deep, bloody imprint of Wacky's beak on his index finger. When I returned home, I could see that Wacky's time with us had come to an end.

In my search for a new home for Wacky, I contacted bird rescues and clubs. One Saturday, there was an exotic bird show not far from my house, and I attended in the hope that I'd overhear someone whose dream it was to have a beautiful, wacked-out cockatoo.

To my delight, as I was studying a cockatoo who was entered in the show, I eavesdropped on a conversation between the cockatoo's owner and a man who was admiring the bird. He said it was his dream to have a big, beautiful white Sulphur crested cockatoo of his own.

Just as he sighed in resignation that he'd never be able to afford one (they can cost upward of $1,000), I popped up

The first time Rich bent over
to go into the cabinet,
Wacky bit him on his tush.

from behind a cage to grant his wish! His eyes misted over as I told him about the availability of Wacky Bird. He did not seem to be concerned by my totally honest description of Wacky Bir-ir-dee and I was impressed by his determination to work with Rich's nemesis.

We made arrangements for him to come to my house to pick up the bird of *his* dreams – and Rich's nightmares.

Upon meeting Wacky, the man was so overcome with joy that he began to cry. It was really quite a sweet introduction and I felt that all of us could look forward to a better future.

As we were loading the cage into the car, Wacky nailed his savior's thumb through the cage bars and drew a whole mess of blood. I held my breath as the man yanked his thumb from the cage. I feared the deal would be off.

But this man was one determined cockatoo lover. He declined my offer to come into the house to wash the wound and bandage it. He wanted that bad birdie.

Although I told him to please call if he changed his mind, I never heard from him. Thus ended the Era of the Brazen and Boisterous Wacky Bir-ir-dee.

And the Winner Is …

"If any of my animals poop or pee pee on you, you'll win a prize. My animals let 'er rip only on people who are cool and who can take it without getting crazy."

That is how I begin each humane education program.

I've been telling the kids in my classes this for more than twenty years in order to avoid the trauma and teasing that are sure to follow when an animal uses a kid as a toilet.

And it has worked like a charm. Instead of theatrics and cries of "EEEUUUU!!!" I see happy smiles from the lucky kids who get peed or pooped on. In fact, it's amazing how many kids suddenly *hope* the animals choose them just so they can win a small prize, usually nothing more than a plastic trinket.

My favorite memory of this phenomenon occurred when I was passing around some rats in a fourth-grade class at Sullivan Avenue Elementary School in Port Jervis, New York. As the rats went from one child's shoulder to the next, everyone's shirt was staying bone dry and perfectly un-pooped on. But there was one child in the group who really, really wanted to be the cool one; the one who could prove he could take whatever an animal had to give.

All the kids in the room had spit on their shirts in hopes of winning the poop/pee pee prize.

The kid spit on his finger and wiped it on his shirt. Then he loudly announced that the rat had peed on him.

As I walked over to see the evidence, the next kid did the same thing. And the next. Soon, all the kids in the room had spit on their shirts in hopes of winning the poop/pee pee prize.

Seldom fooled by young tricksters, I pointed out that rats don't drink enough to produce that quantity of pee pee.

The whole group was busted. No prizes that day.

Another incident occurred at Mohonk Mountain House, a unique Victorian-era resort in New Paltz, New York. This time, I was doing an evening program with an adult audience. The poop/pee pee rule applies to any group regardless of age, so I opened with my usual caution that animals choose only the coolest of people to use as toilets.

I was showing off a white dove named Pax when the bird apparently spotted the coolest dude in the room, flew to the chosen man's shoulder, landed, then pooped in his lap.

The man was very good natured about it, and he happily selected a lovely glow-in-the-dark spider ring as his prize. He was the envy of all in the audience.

So much so that, after the program, his wife approached me and asked if she, too, could have one of the rings. She said that she and her husband wanted to use the rings when they renewed their wedding vows in a ceremony the next day.

It was my pleasure to accommodate them.

Exactly What Is Happening Here?!

"So, Jan, why do all of your kids have chewed-up shoelaces and jagged rubber trim on their gym shoes?" asked Sister Dressed in White and Never Dirty.

"And why are your gym shoes looking equally shabby?" she sniffed.

I hesitated. These were hard things to explain to a nun who pretty much disapproved of everything.

Apparently, she was not aware of the fact that I and the very kind members of our first grade class at St. Theresa-Visitation Elementary School in Detroit, Michigan, allowed our rabbit, Lucan, the freedom to scamper about the room.

We didn't care if Lucan nibbled and chewed on each pair of our shoes as he hopped around the classroom. So why did Sister Never Dirty?

I sighed, stammered and fessed up. My explanation was met with a condescending scowl.

Sister Never Dirty was kept in the dark about the fact that our class held solemn funerals for all the unfortunate mice found dead in the coat closet following every routine pest control attempt. She also was never told that we buried the dead mice on the playground – complete with tiny

17

We didn't care if Lucan nibbled and chewed
on each pair of our shoes
as he hopped around the classroom,
so why did Sister Never Dirty?

crosses.

That was not the only school where I faced interrogation over the various little bits of destruction that can sometimes occur when animals are in our midst.

At St. Mary's Elementary School in Royal Oak, Michigan, I was often asked by parents, "What's with the holes on the corner of each of my child's assignments?" or "Why is my child bringing home papers that look like they were chewed on?"

Hard questions. I tried my best to make the answer sound normal.

Sibley, the class pet cockatiel, could do the answering, but he always sat innocently silent on my desk while I tried to explain.

"Well," I'd begin. "This is Sibley. He's our certification bird."

Uh huh. And what might that be?

Further explanation was in order.

"See, all anyone has to do is hold a piece of paper in front of him, and he uses his beak to poke a ragged hole in it. It's as though he's certifying that the work is properly completed and meets with his approval."

Uh huh. Of course. Doesn't every teacher have a certification bird?

The kids got a big kick out of it, Sibley enjoyed the attention, and each hole of approval produced small paper crumbs that scattered all over my desk and the floor.

Naturally, I was the sole member of the clean-up committee at the end of each day.

Any more questions? No? Then class dismissed.

Teaching a child not to step on a caterpillar is as valuable to the child as it is to the caterpillar.

- Humane Farming Association

We Don't Have Tarantulas, Right?
(I'm Right, Right?)

It was my husband Rich on the phone.

I was away visiting my family in Detroit, Michigan. He was calling from home.

"We don't have any tarantulas in the house, do we?"

He sounded very hopeful that the answer would be no. He said he was only asking because our six-year-old nephew Eric was at the house.

"Eric is here and he says he wants to see the tarantulas, but I told him I didn't think we had any. We don't, right?"

And that's when Rich found out that we did, indeed, have a tarantula in the house. Not roaming around, I assured him. It was living in our designated bird, reptile, amphibian and invertebrate room – a room that he never, ever entered.

Yes, he was creeped out. And yes, he asked me to please let him know when I bring a new resident into our home. I said that I would.

It's actually better now that Rich is aware of every creepy crawly critter in my collection. Now that he knows we have such a variety, he saves his banana peels and over-ripe fruit for the millipedes; he offers me wilted Romaine lettuce leaves for the stick bugs; he keeps stale Cheerios for the rats and strawberry tops for the lizards and tortoises.

As firm believers in the concept of recycling, this makes us very happy.

Still, I think Rich would rather not have any tarantulas in the house.

A very humbling tarantula incident occurred when I was presenting a program to a class of second-graders.

As usual, the kids were taken aback when I took out the exoskeleton (the outer shed or molt) of my tarantula. The shed looks exactly like the actual spider and generally makes people jump back or gasp when they see it on my hand. I always assure the group that, since it isn't alive, it can't move and it won't jump at or hurt them in any way.

The day I was doing the presentation for the second-graders was particularly hot and muggy. An oscillating fan was working hard to keep the classroom cool.

Just as I was promising the class that the tarantula shed couldn't jump or attack them, the fan moved my way. Suddenly, the exoskeleton blew out of my hand and onto the desk of the child seated in front of me.

The child screamed in panic. I quickly retrieved the exoskeleton.

I apologized and reassured the shaken boy, but the rest of the class glared at me throughout the rest of the presentation. They just *knew* I was a complete liar since I promised that something that wasn't alive couldn't jump or go after them.

Do you think they believed anything else I said that day? No. Probably not a word of it.

Eric is here and he says
he wants to see the tarantulas,
but I told him I didn't think we had any.
We don't, right?

I'm right, right?

The Wheeze

Nothing compares to the beauty, grace and gentle cooing of a white dove. Truly, a dove is the perfect symbol of love, peace, purity, serenity and tranquility.

And then there's *Wheezer*.

This odd, little feathered comedian was born in our home, appropriately enough, on Halloween 2009. His father was Pax, a dove who had been the star of my education show until he retired at the age of seventeen.

Pax had been hand-raised by Stephanie and Bill Streeter, directors of the Delaware Valley Raptor Center in Milford, Pennsylvania. They offered to raise the Son of Pax because I don't have the skills necessary for hand-raising baby birds, and I jumped at the offer.

One week after hatching, I sent the featherless imp off to Stephanie for hand-raising, just as she had done with Pax. She would send him back to me when he was fully feathered and no longer being fed dove gruel with an eye dropper.

Wheezer was a very demanding and dramatic infant. He followed Stephanie everywhere she went around the house. He was exposed to the sounds of the kitchen, office, living room, bathroom, television, vacuum cleaner and doorbell. He was truly on his way to becoming a house dove.

His name derived, not surprisingly, by a noise he made. Wherever he happened to be when he grew hungry, Wheezer made his hunger known with a pitiful, wheezing sound. Stephanie would whip up a watery, unappetizing batch of baby dove formula for him and, as she stirred, she would invariably comment to Bill, "The little wheezer is hungry again."

Once he was successfully eating on his own, the Wheeze was returned to me. I was happy to have him back, but it wasn't long before I saw that Wheezer was – to say the least – a bit eccentric.

Early on, I discovered that he was just crazy about the color blue. Anything blue, whether animate or inanimate, qualified as Wheezer's newest love interest. He would be overjoyed at the sight of a blue bucket, a water bottle, a cell phone, an air freshening product – anything, just as long as it was blue.

It was love at first sight, and he would do a full-blown mating dance, bouncing over to the new object of his affection. Then he would bow, coo, peck and finally mount the new blue girlfriend, whether it was the blue top of a peanut butter jar or a blue mug.

The total lack of response he got never seemed to faze him. I suppose he figured the blue phone or bucket would come around to his way of thinking in due time.

Eventually, Wheezer expanded his horizons. He soon was trying to mate with every other animal in the house, regardless of color. If the animal was new to him, he became infatuated and tried to win its affection. Lizards, cats, dogs, tortoises, hermit crabs – all species were game. He also fancied stuffed animals and puppets, ceramic

When the police officer
arrived and I let her into the
house, Wheezer promptly
jumped onto her boot and started to court her.

figurines and the blades of the ceiling fan (happily, only when they weren't rotating).

Wheezer was and remains an insatiable Casanova.

Often when I'm on the phone, Wheezer starts cooing. His slow "Hoo hoo" followed by a rapid fire "Hoohoohoohoohoohoohoo" is well known to my regular callers. Even people who haven't met him will tell me to say hi to the Wheeze.

However, by the end of a conversation when the novelty has worn off, the person on the other end of the line often asks how I can put up with his constant commentary.

"It's just part of the symphony that I call home," I explain.

On one occasion, I accidentally dialed 911 when I meant to dial area code 914. Surprised and embarrassed when the police answered, I apologized and explained my dialing error.

Just as I was assuring the police that there was no emergency, Wheezer began loudly "Hoohoohooing." The dispatcher asked who was screaming in the background. I explained that it was a dove and that everything was really okay.

Well, the police had to be sure. When the officer arrived and I let her into the house, Wheezer promptly jumped onto her boot and started to court her. The officer was a good sport about it and, happily, the Wheeze was not taken into custody.

Wheezer has become one of the most popular and endearing of my animals. Audiences found him irresistible during presentations, and people often offered up their own blue objects for his approval.

More than once, people who had seen him in a previous program showed up at another presentation wearing blue or carrying along a blue doodad for the Wheeze.

One thing is for certain about Wheezer – he makes a memorable impression. Who could possibly forget a dancing, bobbing, cooing dove who loves the color blue?

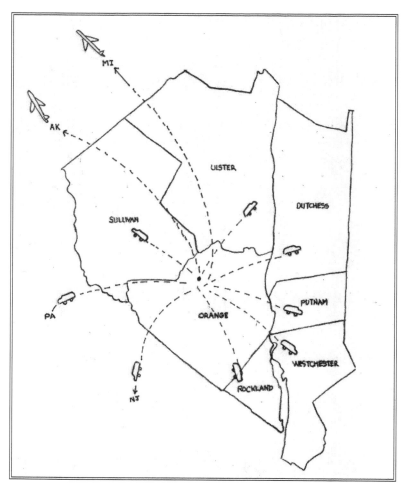

Humane Education on the Move

Taking animals on the road for education programs is not for the faint of heart! For the most part, I travel with my menagerie by car to schools and other venues throughout the Hudson Valley, Delaware Valley and Catskill Mountains in New York and across state borders to nearby Pennsylvania and New Jersey. I have also taken to the sky with my animals to places as far off as Alaska.

Turtle on the Plane

Michael loved turtles. Plain and simple.

But he didn't really know much about them. Michael was one of my teenaged students at H.I. Technical school, a rehab facility for adults with closed-head injuries in Milford, Pennsylvania.

He had grown up on city streets and was unaware that kissing a snapping turtle could give him more than germs. So when Michael picked up a young snapper, he learned an invaluable lesson the hard way.

The turtle grabbed his upper lip and held on fast. I'm not sure how he got it off, but there must have ensued a struggle. When I saw him the day after the incident, his lip was extremely swollen and discolored.

Apparently, having a snapper on his lip did nothing to diminish his desire to own a pet turtle. I assured him I'd try to find one that was captive bred. I explained that it wasn't acceptable, for many reasons, to take animals from the wild and confine them.

A few days later, I flew to Detroit for a visit. While I was there, I went to a pet shop that specializes in captive-born reptiles. They had a box turtle who wasn't in the best of shape. The store owner told me that if I wanted to nurse him back to health, the turtle was mine for free.

I took the turtle and went straight to a veterinarian, who gave me medication for the turtle and put him on a special diet. My job was to use a small spatula the vet gave me to force the turtle's mouth open. Then I had to squirt the medicine and the mushy food into his mouth.

I became relatively skilled at the task during my vacation, but when it was time to fly home and get that turtle to Michael, I had to figure out how to smuggle him into the airplane cabin rather than have him fly in the baggage compartment. He would need his meds and food during the flight.

Airline policy was that only cats and dogs could travel in the cabin. Turtles were not mentioned in the official policy, but it was obvious they were not included among the elite travelers.

Every problem has a solution. At least that's *my* official policy. I figured if I wore a baggy sweatshirt, (defying my sense of style), I could put the turtle in the sleeve and keep him hidden while boarding the plane.

This was well before 9/11, and security was far less stringent in those days. The airline scanners were looking for metal and sharp objects, not turtles. No pat-downs, no wands, no shoes off. Boarding went smoothly.

I sat in a row of three seats by myself, something else unheard of on today's over-crowded flights. There was only one man seated in the row across the aisle from me, too. I relaxed and took a few deep breaths.

About forty-five minutes into the flight, it was time for the turtle's treatment. I set up the food and medicine on the tray table. Then I maneuvered the turtle in my sleeve so that his head and front legs were near the cuff. As I held him through the sleeve, I put the tiny spatula into his mouth, then used an eyedropper to deliver the medication and food.

I suspect the gentleman across the aisle must have wondered why I was putting a spatula and then an eyedropper into my shirt sleeve. Lucky for me he did not buzz for the flight attendant. He probably just figured it was best to ignore me.

In today's world I never would have gotten away with such a stunt. Nor would I have gotten away with bringing a lizard on a plane to Alaska, as I did in 1992. For that particular journey, I tucked the lizard under my hair on the back of my neck. Once on the plane, I opened my purse and the lizard jumped right in for the remainder of the ride.

A very comfortable and uneventful flight for all.

If I wore a baggy sweatshirt,
I could put the turtle in the
sleeve and keep him hidden
while boarding the plane.

People's pets are their own private garden. Even when people cannot communicate with others, they can communicate with animals.

- Count Bernard de Claviere d'Hust

Lap Bunny

I was a passenger in the car during a ride back to the home office of the Living Science Foundation in Novi, Michigan. I had just finished a school program, so there were a few animals in the car with us.

Don't ask me why I do things like this, but I decided to take Aggie, an Angora rabbit, from her carrier and allow her to sit on my lap. She got comfortable and fell asleep. I closed my eyes and also fell asleep.

Not for long, though. I was abruptly awakened by the sensation of something very warm and wet running down my legs, between my legs, and onto the car seat. Ms. Bunny had relieved herself as she lounged on my lap, and I was now sitting in a warm pool of rabbit pee.

I grabbed a roll of paper towels from the back seat and began blotting up liquid from my legs and the seat of the car. Then I began shoving towels down my pants.

As soon as we got to the office, I ran to the bathroom and took off my pants and underwear. I washed both items and laid them on a space heater to dry. I hung out in the bathroom while I waited – where could I possibly go sans pants?

I had to attend a staff meeting later on, and I just hoped my clothing would be dry before I had to leave the bathroom for the meeting. The space heater was turned to the highest setting and, luckily, my slacks dried quickly.

Unluckily, the underwear – which was some kind of nylon blend – melted on the space heater and became very crisp and stiff. Alas, I had no choice but to peel them off the heater and put them back on.

I squirmed uncomfortably throughout the meeting as my itchy, crispy underpants dug into my skin. The lesson I learned from this escapade was that nylon and space heaters are not a good combination.

Don't ask me why I do things like this,
but I decided to take Aggie from her carrier
and allow her to sit on my lap.

Uh-Opossums

"Help!" said the voice on the phone.

Normally when someone is shouting "Help" into a phone, you might think fire. Or robbery. Or maybe someone fell down a well.

You don't usually think opossum. Who has an opossum emergency? But that seemed to be why the owner of a pet shop in upstate Binghamton, New York, was calling me.

"We have five yawari opossums that were rejected by a zoo here," the woman said. "The zoo wanted brush-tailed opossums – not yawaris. And yawaris are what we've got."

She was looking for a home for them. Since I have a soft spot for opossums (and who doesn't, I might ask), I took the two-hour trek northwest to check out these young South American marsupials. Yawaris are a sleeker and browner animal than the fluffier, greyer Virginia opossums that we have in North America.

When I got a look at the five homeless opossum babies, I agreed to take one of them. I immediately narrowed my choice down to the two who were each missing an ear after losing battles with the largest of the group.

They were adorable.
and the fact that
they were one-eared
made them ideal
for my programs.

They were adorable and the fact that they were one-eared made them ideal for my programs. I always look for the less-than-perfect animals to promote my philosophy of respect for all life – with or without blemishes.

I put the two of them on my shoulders and took a stroll around the pet store while deciding which one to take. They treated me like a human tree, racing up and down, hanging from the strap of my shoulder bag, climbing in and out of my purse.

They finally quieted down and seemed to be relaxing on the strap of my purse. How nice and calm they are, I thought. And that's when I heard a loud exclamation:

"Ewww, they're pooping in your pocketbook!"

Now, *there's* a phrase you never want to hear! I looked down to see both babies relieving themselves into my open purse. The runny goo covered everything – key chain, wallet, cell phone, address book, glasses, make-up bag, gum and more.

I asked for the use of the store sink and soap. I emptied the purse onto the counter, cleaned and disinfected everything, then returned all but the gum to the clean but wet purse.

Well, naturally the opossums and I were bonded now. Who wouldn't be after such a warm and intimate introduction. How could I possible choose between them?

I couldn't, of course. I left the shop with two imperfect yawaris and a very imperfect purse.

Sigh.

Kindness is the language which the deaf can hear and the blind can see.

- Mark Twain

Blind Trust
Three Stories about Animals with Impaired Vision

See No Evil – Or Anything Else

When I was in college and still living at home, the world's most compassionate mother – mine – gave me permission to babysit for a blind cat for the weekend. The cat's owner would be out of town and she didn't want to leave her disabled cat alone.

Although I wasn't permitted to have pets of my own, my mom wouldn't say no to a temporary visitor in need (human or otherwise). She suggested our downstairs bathroom as a fine place to set the cat up with all of its necessities.

I brought the short-haired, black and white cat home and took her carrier into the basement. I methodically set out her food, water, toys and bed. I played with her for a while with great pleasure and then, knowing she'd be comfortable, I went upstairs to work on a term paper.

"It has no eyes!" she screamed.

As I closed the door, I assured her I'd be back soon. I wasn't sure she believed me, but I tried to make her feel that all would be fine.

Upstairs, I sat down at the typewriter (fine, yes – a typewriter! – I was in college in the mid-'70s and that's what we used). Almost immediately, I was startled by my mother's scream, which reverberated throughout the house.

"It has no eyes!" she screamed. "You just said it was blind – you didn't tell me it had no eyes in its sockets!"

I ran downstairs to find my traumatized mother juggling a small plate with some tuna fish on it. She thought she'd give the cat a treat and welcome her to her weekend getaway. It never occurred to me that my mom would go down to visit the cat without me, so I hadn't yet told her about the missing eyes.

As it happens, the missing eyes were the result of a self-inflicted wound. When she was a kitten, she'd been abandoned by her mother and had to be hand fed. On one occasion, the kitten got so excited at the sight of her bottle, that she flailed her sharp-nailed paws too close to her eyes and actually scratched them out.

After regaining her composure, my mom reached out to pet the grotesque yet gentle feline. She wished her well and went upstairs to make a few phone calls – each one beginning with, "It has no eyes! Jany just said it was blind – she didn't tell me it had no eyes in its sockets!"

For the next forty years, I would be haunted by that phrase whenever a family discussion turned to the subject of pets.

Iris Had No Irises

Many years later, I adopted a hairless rat who also had no eyes in her sockets.

I named her Iris because, without eyes, she didn't have any irises of her own.

Iris was one of the best rats I ever had. Although she was generally considered by most to be unattractive, she seemed oblivious to the rude stares. She was fearless, friendly, intelligent and soft as warm pizza dough, winning over both kids and adults wherever she went.

In fact, Iris was so popular that she was crowned Queen of the Realm during her coronation ceremony at an after-school program in Port Jervis, New York.

She was the perfect embodiment of humane education — an unattractive, generally shunned and feared creature who won over her former detractors and became both beloved and respected.

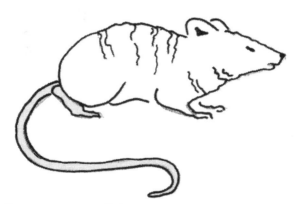

Iris was one of the best rats I ever had.

Mikey Bumps Along

Mikey, the abandoned white poodle, didn't start out blind, but at around the age of seven he developed progressive retinal atrophy, a genetic condition commonly found in white, apricot and gray poodles.

Mikey was a very special dog in Port Jervis, New York, where he traveled to schools with me for many years. Together, we visited all of the elementary school classes each month. Even today, many years later, I run into some former students – now adults – who remember the profound impact of that blind dog.

I lovingly nicknamed him Pinball because, much like the game, he would bounce off an object and continue on his way.

When Mikey started losing his vision, the kids would talk to him and attempt to direct him around rooms and hallways so he could avoid bumping into things. Even with all of the good-natured assistance, though, Mikey still managed to bump into things. He moved very slowly so he never hurt himself. When he took a bump, he'd back up and continue on his way.

I lovingly nicknamed him Pinball because, much like the game, he would bounce from and object and continue on his way.

Based on some very unsettling behavior when I was out of Mikey's ear shot, he became the inspiration for the term "spite poop." Whenever I left the room, a nervous Mikey would twirl, whine and whimper. Then, in his panic, he would conjure up a turd - a welcome back gift, just for me.

Yes, Mikey left his mark on all hearts and many floors of those who knew him.

The Devil's Daughters

A ferret who was blind in one eye also became a member of my menagerie.

Toeser had no trouble getting into trouble with her sister, Linkette, who was fully sighted. These two tricksters collectively earned the name Devil's Daughters as they were in constant motion, running around the house stealing anything that they thought they might need.

My belongings disappeared with great regularity. It wasn't until I was moving to a new home that I discovered – tucked away up inside the bottom lining of a couch – one slipper, a key ring (with keys), a Christmas ornament, a cat toy, a dog biscuit, a brush, a few coins and a variety of other items that I had thought were lost forever.

Clearly, they did not feel any need to ask permission before taking what they deemed essential.

I made this discovery while I was working as the humane educator at the Port Jervis/Deerpark Humane Society. At one point during my time there, I brought a cat home who was due to have kittens so I could keep a close eye on her. Shortly after I brought her into the house, she started to give birth. The ferrets and I watched with great interest as the kittens were born.

The cat was a very good mother and cleaned each of her four babies and relaxed as they nursed. Just as they all settled in, my phone rang and I turned to answer it. When I turned my attention back to the cat family, I noticed there were only three kittens in the bed.

The ferrets were gone and so was a newborn kitten.

It had all happened in a split second, so I knew they couldn't have gone far with their kidnapped kitty. I began a frantic search – under the bed and in the bathroom first. I finally looked behind the bookcase and there were the ferrets, rolling the kitten back and forth between them in a game of their own invention.

To my great relief, the baby looked no worse for wear, and I gently picked her up and placed her back where she belonged. I then put the mischievous ferrets where they couldn't annoy any other critters – at least for a little while.

Ferret cages are only for temporary restraint because ferrets are much too industrious to fare well in a cage for long. They are constantly on the move, and they keep themselves and their owners very, very busy.

They are like kittens who never grow up – the Peter Pans of the animal world. Mine were absolutely fearless and had no problem riding the vacuum cleaner while all other pets ran for cover when I turned it on.

On one special occasion I walked into the room to find each ferret latched on and hanging limp from my dog Pim's ears as he tried desperately to shake them off. It may have been their idea of a carnival ride in Ferretland; however, I immediately put an end to their game and carefully removed each dangling ferret earring from Pim.

The ferrets were gone and so was a newborn kitten. I finally looked behind the bookcase and there were the ferrets, rolling the kitten back and forth between them in a game of their own invention.

Ferrets have a distinctive musky odor that remains even after they groom themselves. Although they keep themselves clean, they don't care much for keeping your house tidy. They use any natural or furniture made corner as a public restroom. They do so by facing away from the corner, then backing up to make their deposit.

I once walked into a house for the first time where I was picking up an unwanted bearded dragon and saw sheets of paper towel tucked into every corner.

"Do you have ferrets as well as lizards?" I asked.

"Yes, we do. How did you know?"

Just a hunch.

As hostesses, my ferrets were dismal failures. When my cousin Howard from Detroit visited me in New York, he was awakened by one of the Devil's Daughters when she ran up his pajama leg and nipped him on the rear.

When my brother-in-law Sam was in town, the two ferrets burrowed into his suitcase and rearranged his neatly packed toiletries.

And when my forever friend Vivienne visited, they helped themselves to one of her brand new shoes, snacking on it while she ate her breakfast.

Anyone who's ever watched ferrets for any length of time is familiar with their little ritual dance (the weasel war dance). They can move forward and backward at the same fast speed and seem to laugh at you as they move backward. I perfected the dance myself and my nephew Josh and niece Loni would often request that I do the "ferret dance" when I visited them in Detroit.

Of course, having no shame, how could I refuse?!

Ferrets can certainly test your patience and composure, no question about it. But if you are armed with a sense of humor, no animal will give you more to laugh about.

Magical Moment
at Mohonk Mountain House

Hedgehogs are round by design and because Miss Hedda Quills was a very good eater, she was rounder than most.

So when I picked her up to place her in her carrier, there was no reason for me to suspect that she could possibly be pregnant.

"We've got to put you on a diet," I told her.

Although I had both a female and a male (Quillbur) hedgehog, they had lived together in a free roaming ten-foot by twenty-foot habitat for more than two years without showing any visible signs of romance. In fact, they barely acknowledged each other. They ate, slept and ran in their wheels as though living parallel lives in separate universes.

Today it was Miss Hedda Quills' turn to be a star in my program at Mohonk Mountain House in New Paltz, New York.

Before bringing out a hedgehog during a program, I always discuss the differences between hedgehogs and porcupines. The audiences at Mohonk are great participants, and they were eager to see which of the two

As I reached into the carrier and picked up
Miss Hedda Quills, I discovered four tiny,
pink bug-like offspring beneath her.

animals – hedgehog or porcupine – would be my mystery guest.

Well, as it turned out, I had five mystery guests that evening. As I reached into the carrier and picked up Miss Hedda Quills, I discovered four tiny, pink bug-like offspring beneath her. Apparently, she had given birth enroute to Mohonk because her new family was already polished and comfortably feeding by the time I got involved. The babies began squeaking in alarm as I lifted their mother from them.

The audience saw the look of astonishment on my face.

Finally, I blurted out the birth announcement.

Everyone at the program was eager to take a peek at the new hedgehog family. And then out came the cameras.

The newborn hedgies' first photo shoot commenced as word spread throughout Mohonk, and the delighted hotel guests converged on the nursery.

Indie
aka
Grand Champion Empress
Indecent Exposure of My Rosebud

A Mohonk Legend

Indie, a Sphynx (hairless) cat, is one of the more docile and compliant of my animal ambassadors.

Prior to my adopting her, Indie had been a grand champion show cat (aka Grand Champion Empress Indecent Exposure of My Rosebud). As a result, she was quite comfortable in large crowds and had no trouble posing for photos and working the audience.

She was with me during a program for Mohonk's Kids Club.

I ended the presentation with a rubber stamp craft. Each child was given paper, ink and animal-themed rubber stamps. The stamps, of course, were meant to be used on the paper, not an animal.

Most of the kids got the idea. Most, but not all.

Little did I realize until it was too late that one small child, who appeared to be doing nothing more than cuddling with Indie on the floor, was in fact applying inked stamps to the cat's naked back and ample belly.

Our tattooed feline became an instant Mohonk legend as her photo went viral on hotel guests' cell phones.

Monkey Business

Larry Friedman had just adopted a squirrel monkey.

The monkey was a product of a couple's recent divorce, and he was quite nervous and shy.

Larry – a photographer from Port Jervis, New York, and a humane society supporter – was a little nervous, too. He asked me to help him acclimate the monkey to his new home. Not knowing what I was in for, I agreed.

I should have been a little nervous, too.

Larry loved monkeys and had built two large enclosures at the back of his photography studio/shop to house two others that he'd previously adopted. For the time being, the new monkey was living in the cage he'd arrived in. Larry would get a new enclosure for him once the monkey felt more comfortable in his new surroundings.

Larry's love for animals did not stop at monkeys. He also had a Vietnamese pot-bellied pig and a gray shelter cat wandering around the studio.

The pig and cat worked as a well-coordinated team to knock over and eat from a snack food counter display that was set up in the back room behind Larry's photo shop. The cat would jump on the counter and knock over the display, then the pig would tear open the bags and they would share the feast. The monkey spent much of his time watching the antics of the pig and cat.

On the day I arrived to see how I could help, the new monkey was out of his cage and investigating the storeroom. He would leap from a counter onto the pig, the cat, the floor and – eventually – onto my head.

I thought it was pretty cute until the cat knocked over the snack display box, the box hit a garbage can lid, the lid noisily hit the floor, and the freaked-out monkey grabbed onto to me with his hands, feet, tail and teeth!

His teeth were so small and sharp that I didn't even feel the bite that had penetrated my jaw. I didn't realize I was bitten until I saw blood running down the front of my shirt. I went into the bathroom to see what was going on. My reflection in the mirror looked like a victim in a slasher movie.

Blood was pouring from my lower jaw.

Larry was horrified and offered to take me to the emergency room. I wasn't in pain and the blood flow was slowing down, so I decided to go home and take care of it myself.

A doctor lived in my housing complex, so I knocked on his door and asked if he thought I would need stitches. He said if I didn't get stitched up, the bleeding would eventually stop, but scar tissue would form on the outside of my face. I decided a trip to the ER would be a good idea.

Not right away, though. I was hungry.

Plus, I was concerned that I might develop lock jaw from the bite and might not be able to eat pretty soon, so I figured I should eat while I could. I went home and made myself a sandwich on a bagel before going to the hospital. I

I didn't realize I was bitten until I saw blood
running down the front of my shirt.

held a towel to my jaw while I prepared and ate the sandwich.

Then I made my way to the ER.

While the doctors and my friends and family questioned my priorities following the monkey bite, I knew how cranky I would be without something to eat. At the time, based on my limited knowledge of the time span between infection and symptoms (from a few days to several weeks, according to the Mayo Clinic), I felt my actions were totally justified and sensible. Now, of course, I wouldn't feel so inclined to stop for a sandwich with a gaping wound in my face.

It all worked out okay, though.

***

On another occasion, I was at Larry's photo shop on humane society business and foolishly stopped in front of a spider monkey's cage. My back was turned to the demon inside.

As I was talking to Larry, the monkey slipped his lengthy tail through the bars of his enclosure. Before I knew what was happening, he wrapped it around my neck and pulled me against the cage bars.

I had to use both hands to unwrap the tail and free myself from its grasp.

Larry found it amusing. I found it reason to stay away from his monkey friends once and for all. As amusing as monkeys are, they clearly do not make great pets.

Confinement is not fair to them. And keep in mind that they fling their poo, and they keep their hands soft and supple by urinating on them.

Kinda makes sharing a meal with them less than appetizing, huh.

Hero Chameleons

Chameleons have always held a particular fascination for me.

Their prehensile tails and turret eyes, their ability to alter colors and patterns, their claw-like fused fingers – all of these characteristics add up to make them seem other-worldly.

A chameleon's sticky-tipped, elastic-like tongue can zap a bug and pull it into his mouth faster than the eye can follow. And it was this amazing tongue that earned Yoshi, a panther chameleon, a place of honor at the Montgomery Village Pharmacy in Montgomery, New York.

I was driving Yoshi home from a veterinary appointment where he had been treated for a broken front leg. He had broken his leg when he attempted to get into the enclosure belonging to Dawn, a female panther chameleon who he was wooing. Even chameleons do dumb things when they're in love.

The vet put Yoshi's forearm into a cast, then covered it with brightly colored gauze to match his vibrant turquoise and blue scales.

I had to stop at the pharmacy on my way home. When I entered, I found that most of the staff members were frantically swatting at two annoying flies behind the counter. Armed with fly swatters, rolled newspaper and a roll of paper towels, the employees were relentless in their attempts to stop the flies from buzzing about.

Lucky for them, I was chauffeuring the ultimate flycatcher.

I offered to retrieve Yoshi from the car and bring him in to save their sanity. Desperate for relief, they readily agreed to have me bring in the expert.

Yoshi was still a bit wobbly from his veterinary experience; however, he was able to balance himself on the sink behind the front counter. He knew exactly what was expected of him.

With the pharmacy staff and customers watching in anticipation, Yoshi's rotating eyes zeroed in on the flies. Within seconds, he snapped them up and devoured them.

The grateful staff applauded. When the cheering died down, one customer said she was disappointed that her daughter, who found waiting for prescriptions too boring, had chosen to stay in the car.

Too bad for her. Due to her impatience, she missed the one-time-only performance of the fly-catching ace.

Yoshi's love interest, Dawn, showed off her own fly-catching expertise at Heritage Feed, a local animal supply store in Bullville, New York. I had gone in for some dog food and found that a small swarm of flies was hanging around in front of the cash register.

I immediately turned around and went home to get Dawn, my all-natural bug zapper who was a whiz at snapping flies right out of air. Within seconds of placing

With the pharmacy staff and customers
watching in anticipation,
Yoshi's rotating eyes zeroed in on the flies.
Within seconds, he snapped them up
and devoured them.

her on the counter, Dawn performed her magic – and not a fly was left to tell the story.

Once again, staff and customers were amazed by the exterminating accuracy of the chameleon, and store history was made.

All who were there that day will attest to the fact that heroes come in many forms – just as chameleons do.

It's nice to be important, but it's more important to be nice.

- Norma Berlin

The Mystery of Marshmallow

In all the years I've taken shelter cats to schools for humane education programs, none has ever left the car before actually *arriving* at the school.

That is, not until Marshmallow, the orange tiger cat who would eventually be nicknamed Houdini, for reasons that will become clear.

One cool spring afternoon when I was on my way to an elementary school with Marshmallow, I decided to make a quick stop at Wells, a family-owned candy and paper supplier, to pick up some items they were holding for me.

I had all four windows open a crack as I drove to the store. Marshmallow was contentedly stretched out on the back seat of the car, enjoying the breeze while basking in the sun.

I parked the car in front of the store. Marshmallow didn't seem to notice as I left the vehicle. He was asleep, and I figured he'd be in the exact same position when I returned to the car.

While I was paying for the items at the register, the clerk and I both heard pleading meows coming from a location

How had he been able to squeeze his adult cat
body through a cracked window?

that we couldn't identify. We exchanged confused looks, then looked around us for the source of the plaintive cries.

Finally, we looked toward the front glass door. We were astonished to see Marshmallow sitting there, apparently crying to be let inside. I opened the door, and in he sauntered.

What was so puzzling was that Marshmallow chose exactly the right door to find me. How did he know which door on the block was the one where he would be welcomed?

Why didn't he bolt for freedom or into one of the many backyards on the block?

And – the biggest mystery of all – how had he been able to squeeze his adult cat body through a cracked window? Unfortunately, it wasn't caught on tape, so I'll never know.

What I do know is that, shortly after this mysterious adventure, Marshmallow/Houdini was lucky enough to be adopted by an intuitive nurse who was fascinated by his back story and felt that the adoption was destined to happen.

She provided him with a spacious home on a placid lake with a panoramic view. And she promised to never leave the door open, not even a crack.

Doves Cooed, I Drooled

As I walked to my car from the home of a family who had just adopted two baby white doves from me, I couldn't help but wonder what had caused them to glance back and forth at each other during my visit.

I had met a few members of this family several days earlier at my annual fund raising yard sale. They had immediately been taken with the baby doves and inquired about adoption.

I told them they needed to do some research on the care of doves. They also needed to invest in the appropriate kind of cage and supplies.

They were excited and said they would contact me when they were set up to provide a proper home for these delightful birds.

When I got the call that they were ready for the doves, I told them I had a dental appointment that afternoon and would deliver the birds afterward. As promised, I brought the babies to their new home. Once again, I met the grandmother, the mother and her three children.

I visited with them for half an hour and answered all of their questions. I chatted along, being my charming self (or so I thought) as I provided them with valuable information

I was impressed with their set up and felt comfortable leaving the birds with the family. What I didn't understand was why they kept exchanging peculiar glances with each other during our entire visit.

and instructions. I was impressed with their set up and felt comfortable leaving the birds with the family.

What I didn't understand was why they kept exchanging peculiar glances with each other during our entire visit.

After I said farewell, I entered my car and fastened the seatbelt. Then I looked into the rear view mirror. To my horror, I discovered I had blood tricking from both corners of my mouth.

I looked like a vampire who had just had a good meal.

The blood was obviously a result of my dental procedure, but what on earth had that family thought? They must have been either too fearful or too polite to ask.

I'll never know. Usually, people who have adopted animals from me stay in contact in order to give me progress reports.

Not surprisingly, I never heard from this family again.

Nice Try!

"We expect you to clean it up!"

So spaketh a member of the Southfield, Michigan, *Cranbrook Place Condominiums* Homeowners Association.

The panel seated before me glared at me while waiting for me to confess that my cute little black Pomeranian, Pim, was the culprit. They seemed to believe that it was Pim who produced the massive layer of poop deposited on – and spread all over – the lawn and walkway in front of the gatehouse to their la-di-da upscale living community.

With defiance burning behind my eyes, I gently hoisted up the accused from his comfortable position on my lap.

"You believe this little five-pound dog is responsible for the field of manure on the walkway and front lawn?" I asked, incredulous.

To my astonishment, they all replied in unison.

"Yes!" they said.

Apparently this renowned committee had not considered that the beautiful grounds with glistening ponds and manicured lawns was a very popular hangout for Canadian

You believe this little five-pound dog is responsible for
the field of manure on the walkway and front lawn?
I asked, incredulous.
To my astonishment, they all replied in unison.
Yes! they said.

geese. These visitors would serenely glide across the ponds, which they considered their own.

Unwilling to soil their own pond water, in which they swam and fed, they chose to defecate on the beautifully mowed lawns instead.

"Goose poop is what all of you have been stepping in, around and through," I told the committee. "Nice try, but my little dog is innocent!"

I then presented the committee with two transparent sandwich bag treasures for their consideration. Exhibit A was marked Goose and Exhibit B was marked Dog.

The difference was clear.

"The clean-up committee will have to be chaired by someone other than me," I told them.

There was nothing left to be said, so Pim and I exited the conference room with great dignity, the untidy matter now resolved.

The greatness of a nation
and its moral progress
can be judged by the way
it treats its animals.

- Mahatma Gandhi

Incoming Bats!

While I was curator at the Hudson Highlands Nature Museum, in Cornwall, New York, a not-to-be-missed opportunity presented itself. The museum was going to be able to acquire three captive born Egyptian fruit bats for a new exhibit.

I was bursting with excitement. Finally, I had a chance to bring my favorite animal species to the museum!

After months of filling out special permit forms and sitting for interviews with appropriate agencies, the three bats finally arrived at Stewart Airport in Newburgh, New York. Because the bats' new habitat at the museum was not yet completed, I had the privilege of taking them home.

They would be temporarily housed in my home office.

In preparation for their arrival, I set up a large nylon and mesh camping tent. I also hung mangoes, berries and bananas inside the enclosure, ready for the bats' arrival. I was pleased with the way everything looked and hoped the bats would find the accommodations comfortable.

As I removed the bats from their traveling box, I carefully hung each one inside the tent by its small

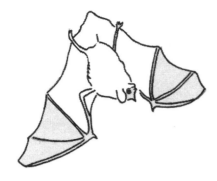

During their industrious nighttime activities, they totally redecorated my office. I was not a big fan of their art work. Sticky fecal matter and fruit chunks were splatted everywhere.

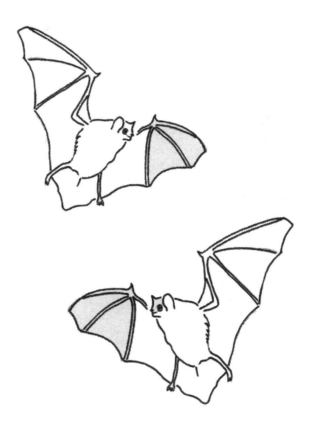

grasping feet. All were placed without incident. I felt confident they would be fine in there overnight.

When I awoke the following morning, though, the reality of housing bats in a flimsy tent became clear. The gaping hole in the top of the tent was my first clue that the bats were not satisfied with the accommodations. It was not enough for them to simply fly around under the big top.

I found the three of them hanging from the light fixtures on the office ceiling.

From that point on, I understood that the bats had taken over my office. It was not to be my own during their visit.

In fact, during their industrious nighttime activities, they totally redecorated my office. Every morning, new colors and textures were slathered on all surfaces. Although Jackson Pollock might have appreciated their artistic endeavors, I was not a big fan of their art work. Sticky fecal matter and fruit chunks were splatted everywhere – all over the walls and even between papers in file folders.

Apparently, with each orbit around the room, the three Musketeers spewed projectile poop. They also flung fruit remnants against the walls and somehow managed to get their mess inside the light fixtures, as well. This behavior is useful in the wild as they replenish forests; however, in the office it's just gross.

After a two-week visit, the museum's bat habitat was ready for them. At last, they were relocated to their permanent home.

Their arrival had been reason for joyous celebration; their departure even more so.

The Flying Squirrel Follies

If you ever find yourself to be the proud owner of a baby flying squirrel, there's only one way to bond with it. Allow it to sleep in a pouch hanging from your neck.

This is how a baby learns to recognize its caretaker.

I recently adopted a baby squirrel to keep my older flying squirrel, Skids, company. Skids was given to me following the death of both his original owner and his squirrel buddy, and I felt he needed a friend.

Flying squirrels can live for fifteen years, and they need social interaction with their own kind in order to thrive. Still, adopting a baby flying squirrel, no matter how worthy the cause, can be a bit of an ordeal.

Before one of my new baby's midnight feedings, I realized that I was close to being out of cream, one of the ingredients for her formula. Although it wasn't that cold out, I wanted to keep the baby warm while we ventured out to the store.

I put on my warmest winter wear – a long, bright red, hooded coat – and carefully buttoned it over the baby squirrel sleeping in the pouch hanging around my neck. I drove to the convenience store on my corner and went in to purchase some cream for the formula.

While I was looking in the dairy case, I felt the baby wake up. She crawled out of the pouch and moved to my shoulder. I didn't want her to squeeze out from under my coat, so I flipped up the hood and started squirming awkwardly. In retrospect, I realize I may have alarmed the midnight clerk in my spastic attempt to adjust myself to prevent the squirrel from leaving the safety of my coat and gliding onto some merchandise.

Above the dairy case, I could see my reflection in the tilted security mirrors that lined the store. I noticed the clerk watching my suspicious behavior in the mirrors. I felt some sort of explanation was in order, so when I got to the register, I tried to explain what was happening.

I realized immediately that he spoke little English. He made no acknowledgment of either the tale I was telling him or the tail that was sticking out from my hood. I'm just grateful he didn't call the police on suspicion that I was shoplifting and stuffing food beneath my coat.

As the baby grew, so did our activities together. During playtime out of the cage, when I was wearing a thick, floor-length terrycloth bathrobe, the squirrels would run up, down and around me, scampering as if they were on a tree.

I kept seeds and nuts in the pockets of the robe, and they would eagerly retrieve them when they crawled into the pockets.

During one of their more adventurous outings, they burrowed under the robe and perched on my tush. Moments later, I felt the waistline of my pajamas snapping repeatedly against my skin.

I was puzzled by this new game and wondered what they were up to. Finally, I noticed seeds and nuts on the floor next to my foot. Ah ha! I realized that every time they opened the waistband, they were dropping a portion of their seed and nut bounty down my pant leg into what they *thought* was a safe hiding place.

Young squirrels have much to learn.

About pajamas, anyway.

I may have alarmed the midnight clerk
in my spastic attempt to adjust myself
to prevent the squirrel from leaving
the safety of my coat.

Princess Tasha

Tasha, a snowshoe Siamese cat, made quite a name for herself in the classrooms of Port Jervis, New York.

Her regal presence was perfect for wowing even the gloomiest of children in a classroom. It was the children in the elementary schools who dubbed her Princess Tasha. They also made the rule that all students were required to bow or curtsy as a group before Tasha would exit her carrier/carriage in each classroom.

An interesting side effect of the classroom bow was that, without instruction, many kids who saw me with her carrier in the hallway would stop to do simple bow before us, then continue silently on their way.

At Sullivan Avenue Elementary School, I did my monthly programs in the multi-purpose room, which had a stage complete with curtains, lights and under-the-stage storage for props.

I'd let Tasha walk around the room during my presentation. She was quite comfortable exploring whatever was on the stage at the time.

On one occasion, I thought nothing of the fact that she was using a delicate white paw to lift a small door under the stage and go underneath to explore. I figured that I'd lift the door at the end of the class and call her out.

Little did I know that under the stage was a network of ventilation duct work that led to every classroom in this very old, two-story building.

When my calls to her were ignored at the end of the class period, I borrowed a flashlight to look around beneath the stage. It was then that I realized she had disappeared into the duct work! I alerted the office. In turn, all the teachers were alerted to be on Tasha Alert.

I received reports of Tasha sightings throughout the day as the cat's head popped up periodically behind the vents in various classrooms.

When it was time to close up the school for the weekend, Tasha was still wandering through the ducts. The custodians and school administrators decided it would be best not to set the school's burglar alarm because it was activated by motion. Tasha, moving non-stop about the building, would be constantly setting it off.

How embarrassed was I? Extremely so!

I tried one last time, to no avail, to get her to come out. Then I left the building. How lucky for me, though, when I heard there was a Boy Scout troop scheduled to meet in the building that night.

With high hopes, I returned to the scene of the disappearance just as the boys arrived for their meeting. I walked into the building armed with a carrier and the stinkiest can of cat food that I could find.

I set up my food trap under the stage and waited. The Scouts remained silent during my stake-out. It didn't take long.

Within about ten minutes, there was Tasha – covered in cobwebs, dust and assorted debris from who knows where? With no apology for her scruffy appearance and no explanation about her disappearance, she glanced over at me and began eating.

Princess Tasha's reign over the school's innards was over. While on her escapade, she had navigated through the ducts of her kingdom. Then, based on her personal itinerary, she made a grand appearance in her own good time.

Motoring On ...

As Tasha's story comes to a close, this leg of our journey has ended.

In spite of all the embarrassments and calamities, I continue my quest to promote the importance of being humane, and I look forward to every new adventure - even those that come with a snafu or two.

- Jan Berlin

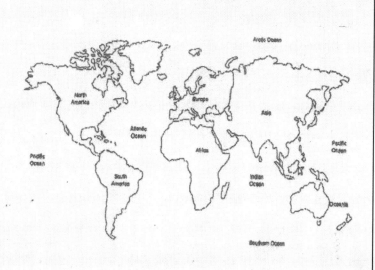

Countries of Origin
(All Ambassadors are captive born in USA)

Legless Lizard - Russia
Lion - Africa
Cockatoo - Australia
Dutch Rabbit - Holland
Cockatiel - Australia
Chilean Rose Tarantula - Chile & Bolivia, So. America
Ring-necked dove - Africa
Box Turtle - Eastern U.S.A.
Angora Rabbit - Turkey, Asia/Europe
Yawari Opossum - So. America/Caribbean
Cat, domestic short hair - U.S.A.
Rat - Norway, Europe
Poodle - Germany, Europe
Ferret - European Polecat -Europe
Pygmy Hedgehog - Africa
Sphynx Cat - U.S.A. & Canada
Monkeys - South America
Chameleons - Madagascar, Africa
Cat, Marshmallow - Domestic Long Hair, U.S.A.
Dove, ring-neck - Africa
Pomeranian Dog - Central Europe
Egyptian Fruit Bats - Egypt
Southern Flying Squirrels - Eastern U.S.A.
Cat, Snowshoe Siamese - U.S.A.

Acknowledgments

How lucky am I to be doing what I'm passionate about, surrounded by people who inspire and encourage me? To those who have contributed to the growth of Everything Animals, I salute you!

My original text was much more specific about everyone listed here. However, there aren't enough pages in the book for that. So here, in chronological order, I thank you for your support.

P.S. If you want to hear what I wrote about you, call me!

In Detroit, Where Human Education Seeds Were Planted

Norma and Al Berlin (nicest parents), Mindy Berlin Herman (best-in-the-world sister), Aunt Shirley (more like a grandmother), Wendy Shepherd (truly the boss of me), Dale Shepherd Dallaire (so generous), Howard Davis, Donna Roth, Suzi Gabe Kellman, Sherry Lowenthal, Les Leider, Sam Herman, Debbie Warsh, Josh Herman, Loni Wildern, Don Griffin, Liz Meyers, Vivienne Manwaring, RWM III.

Growing in Pennsylvania

Pam Brauchli and Amy Ray.

In Full Bloom in New York

Humane Society of Port Jervis/Deerpark (ahead of its time): Lynda and Fred Gerenser, Doris and George Hammond, Stephanie and Bill Streeter, Lynne Tears, Carla Layton, Holly Romahn, and Tia and George Williams.

School Personnel Who Get It: Donna Muro (former principal supreme of Anna S. Kuhl Elementary, Port Jervis), teachers and administrators of the Port Jervis, Minisink and Delaware Valley schools; John Muollo (program director, Club Rec), Deb Smorto and Fields of Green Montessori School; Kate Fox, Ed Helbig and the Birch School.

Reporters and Photographers Who Get It: Tracy Baxter, Amy Berkowitz, Deb Botti, Fina Bruce, Tom Bushey, Mary Esparra, Tom Leek and Beth Quinn.

Museum of the Hudson Highlands (amazing collaborators): Janet Pirog, Jill Gruber and Pam Golben.

Annual Yard Sale Contributors: The Pluchino family (Kelly, Chris, Hailey and Madison), Lynda and Fred Gerenser, Pam and Mark Golben, Doris and George Hammond, Julie Locke, Stephanie and Bill Streeter, Dawn and Steve Finn, Loriann, John and Patrick Lahl, Bob and Andy Murphy, Kate Fox and Ed Helbig, Nicole, Joe, Jacob and Bradley Jurain.

Cheerleaders, Volunteers and Friends: Donna Steffens, Steve, Keith and Daniel Fajfer, Carol Mason and Paul DiMaggio, Roz Shafer, Julie Locke, Sheree Biro, Lynn Howard, Heidi Wagner, Evi Seidman, Tammy Ale, Vanessa Ale, Liz Foxx, Heidi Wagner, Tanya Tyler and Grace Perez.

Parents and Students Who Care: All of the pre-school, home-school and after-school families who have participated and promoted our on-site activities.

New York Libraries That Get It: Ramapo-Catskill Library System and the Mid-Hudson Library System.

Those Who Bring Us to Group and Nursing Homes: Evelyn Cannata, senior recreation therapist at OPWDD, and Debbie Manzo, activities director at Valley View.

Kind Veterinarians: Cedarknoll Animal Hospital (Dr. Terri Greer), Otterkill Animal Hospital (Dr. James Zgoda), West End Veterinary Offfices (Dr. Donald Factor) and Roeder's Ark (Dr. Delores Roeder).

Experts Always Ready to Assist: Jason McKnight (Frankenchams) and Jerry Hillard (Jerry the Snakeman).

Buddies with the Same Passion for Animals: Les Maier, Jeanne Patterson and Diane Sandbothe.

Generous Businesses and Agencies: Stonehenge Farm Market of Bullville, Pine Bush Agway (Elijah Howe), Montgomery Book Exchange, Pampered Pet of Pine Bush (Terri Scott), Petco of Middletown, Walden Savings Bank, Quickway Exotic Auto of Bloomingburg (Vee), Sam's Club of Middletown, Bricks4Kidz of New Windsor, Old's Cool of Bullville (Heather Barnum), Late Bloomer Farms of Montgomery, Orange County Water Authority, Putnam County Children's Expo & Safety Fair, Transitions Hair Studio of Port Jervis (Jody Ritchie), The Craft Show of Milford, Pa (Amy Eisenberg) and Kohl's Mamakating Distribution Center in Wurtsboro (Tom Dolan).

Photography, Website, and EBay Team (unbeatable): Irene Shafer, Justine Monahan, Nicole Jurain, Michael Lewis, and Regina Crespo.

Magnificent Mohonk Mountain House: Entertainment managers Robyn Gullickson, Courtney Stockdale, Cathi Roosa-Tokle, Lee Blake and Amy Sherwood; night manager Steven Dickman; and all the valet guys.

Special Thanks

There would be no Everything Animals Resource & Activity Center, Inc. without the support of my father-in-law, Joseph C. Blazeski, and the encouragement and all-around, every day assistance of my husband, Rich Blazeski.

Who Else Cares?

Apparently you do, judging from the wonderful support Everything Animals has received from people who believe in an organization that cares for the cast-offs.

We support ourselves through a variety of means - program fees, grants, public and private donations, an eBay presence, and the Everything Animals annual yard sale.

Held every Father's Day weekend, our three-day yard sale offers the public a chance to "make a donation and take home a gift."

We let shoppers decide how much to give, and we have found that our local animal lovers are very giving. While a regular yard sale has plenty of haggling, an Everything Animals yard sale has generous patrons who drop something in the donation jar even if they don't find a treasure to take home.

The yard sale is held at 2807 Route 17K, Bullville. If you can't wait until the yard sale to make a donation, please contact us to find out how you can help or send a donation to:

Everything Animals Resource & Activity Center, Inc.
PO 104
Bullville, NY 10915

Phone: 845-361-4465
Email: janimals@warwick.net
Web: everythinganimalsresources.org

Thank you!

About the Authors and Illustrator

Author Jan Berlin has more than thirty-five years of experience teaching in both traditional and non-traditional educational settings. As founder and director of Everything Animals Resource & Activity Center, Inc., she has been able to combine her love of teaching with her passion for humane education and animal welfare advocacy. Jan lives in Bullville, New York, with her husband, Rich Blazeski, and the myriad of animals who have made their way into her heart as well as onto the pages of this book.

Illustrator and co-author Lynda Gerenser, RN, of Huguenot, New York, served as an officer on the board of directors at the Humane Society of Port Jervis/Deerpark for twenty-five years. She continues her dedication to animal welfare and humane education as board president and artistic director at Everything Animals Resource & Activity Center, Inc. Lynda enjoys water color painting and has donated a number of her pieces to local charities for fund raising. She also co-authored the book *Some Days You're the Dog – Some Days You're the Hydrant.*

Be Kind ...

Because Nice Matters

Made in the USA
Charleston, SC
04 March 2016